To: Geneviève (For you & Michael) 12/2002
Love,
Elaine

Love

God's Greatest Treasure

PAINTINGS BY

Sandy Lynam Clough®

HARVEST HOUSE PUBLISHERS
EUGENE, OREGON

I wish for you faith...
I send to you hope...
I share with you love from a joyful heart.

—Sandy Lynam Clough

Love—God's Greatest Treasure

Published by Harvest House Publishers
Eugene, Oregon 97402

ISBN 0-7369-0517-0

Sandy Clough Studios
25 Trail Road
Marietta, GA 30064
1.800.447.8409

Design and production by Garborg Design Works, Minneapolis, Minnesota

Harvest House Publishers has made every effort to trace the ownership of all poems and quotes. In the event of a question arising from the use of a poem or quote, we regret any error made and will be pleased to make the necessary correction in future editions of this book.

Printed in China.

01 02 03 04 05 06 07 08 09 10 / IM / 10 9 8 7 6 5 4 3 2 1

Love is a force more formidable than any other. It is invisible—it cannot be seen or measured, yet it is powerful enough to transform you in a moment, and offer you more joy than any material possession could.

BARBARA DE ANGELIS

Love is more than just a word. It is the common denominator that links us all together no matter what language we speak. It is exemplified in the bond between mother and child, illustrated in the closeness of sisters, and perfected in the sacrifice of our heavenly Father. It can sometimes be the only constant in a storm of chaos. If you look for it, you will surely find it.

Love never fails.

Love comforteth like sunshine after rain.

William Shakespeare

Where there is great love, there are always wishes.

WILLA CATHER

And now these three remain: faith, hope and love. But the greatest of these is love.

THE BOOK OF 1 CORINTHIANS

You will find as you look back upon your life that the moments when you have truly lived are the moments when you have done things in the spirit of love.

HENRY DRUMMOND

Sometimes it is a great joy
just to listen to someone we love talking.

VINCENT MCNABB

A friend is one who knows you and loves you just the same.

ELBERT HUBBARD

The greatest happiness of life is the conviction
that we are loved—loved for ourselves, or rather,
loved in spite of ourselves.

VICTOR HUGO

Treasure the love you receive above all. It will survive long after your good health has vanished.

Og Mandino

It's love that makes the world go round.

ANONYMOUS

Surely goodness and love will follow me all
the days of my life, and I will dwell in the
house of the LORD forever.

THE BOOK OF PSALMS

The King of love my Shepherd is,
Whose goodness faileth never;
I nothing lack if I am His,
And He is mine forever.

SIR H.W. BAKER

Love is the poetry of the senses.

Honoré de Balzac

God loves each of
us as if there were
only one of us.

Saint Augustine

*If I speak in the
tongues of men and of angels,
but have not love, I am only
a resounding gong or a clanging cymbal.*

The Book of 1 Corinthians

People won't care about how much we know until they know how much we care.

CHUCK SWINDOLL

God's love for us is not a love that always
exempts us from trials, but rather,
a love that always sees us through trials.

AUTHOR UNKNOWN

*All, everything that I understand,
I understand only because I love.*

LEO TOLSTOY

Love doesn't make the world go 'round.
Love is what makes the ride worthwhile.

FRANKLIN P. JONES

Love is friendship caught on fire.

Pamela McDuffy

*Let the morning bring me word of your unfailing love,
for I have put my trust in you. Show me the way
I should go, for to you I lift up my soul.*

The Book of Psalms

Whoever loves much, does much.

THOMAS À. KEMPIS

Love is not a matter of counting the years;
It's making the years count.

WILLIAM SMITH

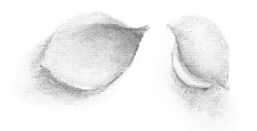

We can do no great things—
only small things with great love.

MOTHER TERESA

The unity that binds us all together, that
makes this earth a family, and all
men brothers and the sons of God, is love.

THOMAS WOLFE

*Greater love has no one than this, that
he lay down his life for his friends.*

THE BOOK OF JOHN

To love is to receive a glimpse of heaven.

KAREN SUNDE

What a man desires is unfailing love...

THE BOOK OF PROVERBS

Love is a fabric which never fades,
no matter how often it is washed in the
waters of adversity and grief.

Anonymous

Love is not getting, but giving.

Henry Van Dyke

Joy is love exalted; peace is love in response; long-suffering is love enduring; gentleness is love in society; goodness is love in action; faith is love on the battlefield; meekness is love in tough situations; and temperance is love in training.

Dwight L. Moody

I never knew how to worship until I knew how to love.

HENRY WARD BEECHER

God is love; and he that
dwelleth in love
dwelleth in God,
and God in him.

THE BOOK OF 1 JOHN

Love is a canvas furnished by nature and embroidered by imagination.

VOLTAIRE

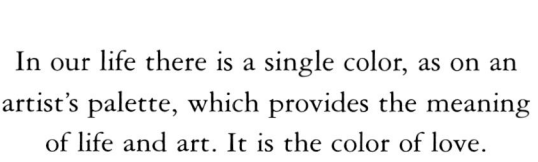

In our life there is a single color, as on an artist's palette, which provides the meaning of life and art. It is the color of love.

MARC CHAGALL

Love will find a way.

Proverb

Love changes darkness into light and makes
the heart take a "wingless flight."

Helen Steiner Rice

*Every time you smile at someone,
it is an action of love, a gift to
that person, a beautiful thing.*

Mother Teresa

Sandy Lynam Clough

Love is a medicine for the sickness of the world; a prescription often given, too rarely taken.

KARL MENNINGER

May no gift be too small to give, nor too simple to receive, which is wrapped in thoughtfulness, and tied with love.

L.O. BAIRD

There is no remedy for love but to love more.

Henry David Thoreau

Love feels no burden, thinks nothing of trouble, attempts what is above its strength, pleads no excuse of impossibility; for it thinks all things lawful for itself, and all things possible.

Thomas À. Kempis

A loving heart is the truest wisdom.

Charles Dickens

Love is the master key which
opens the gates of happiness.

Oliver Wendell Holmes

Love is ever the beginning of knowledge,
as fire is of light.

Thomas Carlyle

Love isn't like a reservoir. You'll never drain it dry.
It's much more like a natural spring. The longer
and the farther it flows, the stronger and the deeper
and the clearer it becomes.

EDDIE CANTOR

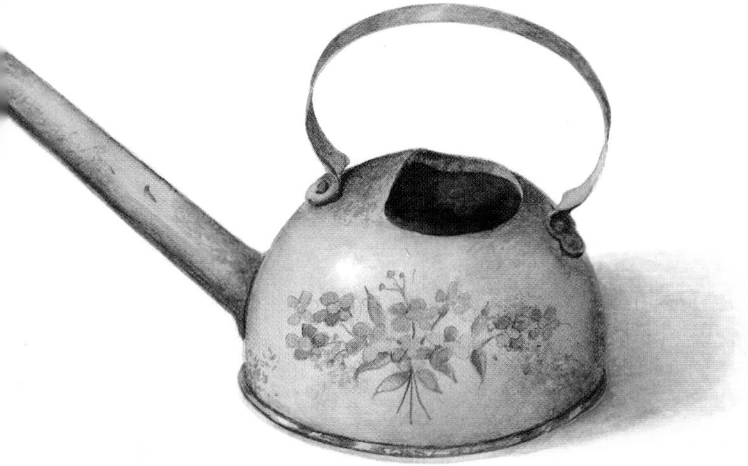

Love does not delight in
evil but rejoices with the truth.
It always protects, always trusts,
always hopes, always perseveres.
Love never fails.

The Book of 1 Corinthians

The honorary duty of a human being is to love.

MAYA ANGELOU

Love, while you are able to love.

A. FRIELIGRATH

If you'd be loved, be worthy to be loved.

Ovid

Love many things, for therein lies the true strength, and whosoever loves much performs much, and can accomplish much, and what is done in love is well done.

Vincent van Gogh

Love for the joy of loving, and not for the offerings of someone else's heart.

Marlene Dietrich

Keep love in your heart. A life without it is like a sunless garden when the flowers are dead. The consciousness of loving and being loved brings a warmth and richness to life that nothing else can bring.

Oscar Wilde

But I will sing of your strength, in the morning I will sing of your love...

THE BOOK OF PSALMS